Lawn Care Business

How to Become Successful in Low Cost Lawn Business

By John Baker

Contents

Introduction 5

Chapter 1-How to Start Lawn Care Business 11

    Your Goals and Mission Statement 11

    Select Your Target Market 12

    Determine Your Services 12

    Flourish Your Skills 13

    Getting Equipment on a Budget 14

    Transportation Costs 16

    Guidance Information 16

    Advertising on a Budget 17

    Other Startup Disbursals 18

    Licensing Your Business 18

    Evaluate to Learn and Grow 19

    Build a Trusted Team 19

    Knowledge about Climate and Plants 20

    Winter Plans 20

    Staying Updated is the Key 21

    Financial Necessities 21

Chapter 2- How to Get Clients 23

    Target Client 23

    Define Your Business for Clients 24

    Enduring the Storm 25

    Advertise to Attract Clients 25

    Working Smarter Not Harder 26

    Time Management 27

Marketing 29

Take Initiatives In Favor Of the Customers 30

Leverage Your Customers 31

Chapter 3- Earn Money in Off Season Lawn Business 33

Conclusion 37

Introduction

Lawn means a flat and a mowed area in front of a house, building or park. Usually, it is covered with green grass. Normally, lawns in front of houses are seen in the European country, mostly, but lawns in front of parks, schools or colleges or even in front of estates are available throughout every continent. If one has a lawn, it is, with no doubt, has to be taken care of. A green bushy lawn is an eyesore for everyone and everything. In order to clean a lawn on a daily or weekly basis, you need to maintain some certain steps. It may feel troublesome, but the outcome is worthy of taking the trouble.

Nowadays, lawn care has turned out to be a fruitful business for people of all ages. Some people consider this as a business out of their own interest in cleaning and maintaining the nature and some take it as a profit based business. Either way, it depends on the subjective point of persuasion to start your own lawn maintenance business. The fresh scent of new cut grass is soothing and intoxicating, but that cannot be the sole reason to prefer the lawn care business or to prepare your yard into a home business store. There are pros and cons of every little thing. When you are starting a business, you obviously have to look at all the pros and cons in an elaborated or detailed way. The best thing about this business is that you can customize it to the customers' demands and needs.

The pros in this business are:

- As lawns need to be cleared once in a week, thus, it makes the business a perennial and an ongoing business. The owner will get calls from his customers on a daily basis to take care of their lawns. The business will flourish immediately and will enjoy busy moments 24/7 throughout the year. You can even make it a part-time source of income. Some teachers, cops, and firemen are known to make more money taking care of lawns and gardens as a part-time gig than they normally do when working full time on their main job.

- Another attractive feature of this business is that, other than the cleaning of the lawns, you will get the chance of taking care of your customers' extra maintenance requirements regarding the lawn in every 4-6 weeks. Extra maintenance means earning extra profits. The lawns need extra attention to get rid of the weed and to destroy the possible threat of having bugs. These extra treatments are consumable as they are a repetitive process; thus, making the business a successful one.

- This business is expandable in size and even in profit. First, you can start out your business with one service that is mowing the lawns. But, later you can expand it to the business of weeding, tree trimming, landscaping services, and gardening and so on according to the demands and needs of the customers. You can serve as many services as possible by setting up just one business and can earn profits easily.

- You can even customize this business according to your needs and expertise. You can be the sole owner of the business and do all the works single-handedly, or you can be the person who manages multiple lawn care business from his home office. This business has a low overhead. For example, if you currently don't have lots of work, then you will not need to pay your workers if you have engaged them per the hour. Imagine, you can even run the entire business from the comfort of your house, hence no need to pay additional rent.

- If you want to expand your business and you feel the need for workers, you can hire as many employees as you need without any worry. The best part of this business is hiring workers, as it doesn't need any special hardcore training to mow the lawn. You will not have to spend extra money for the training part to make your employees learn about the work; which means there are no recruiting expenses that you have to bear.

- If you have any interest in purchasing an existing franchise in the field of lawn business and if you want to start your business from it, there are many reputable and renowned lawn case business franchises are available. The advantages of purchasing the business model from these franchises are you will get their established customers and equipment along with it.

- It involves revenue generating consumables. People will not just want to have their lawns maintained but will also require special treatments and fertilizers for bugs and weeds nearly every 4 to 6 weeks. This is an attractive aspect of your business as such treatments may be viewed as "consumables" due to their reoccurring usage.

- Stepping stone into work that is more profitable. Establishing a solid customer base for your lawn business is an easy pathway for more profitable undertakings like landscape installation, walkways, patios, fences, and sprinklers. You may want to view lawn maintenance as the quick nickels while the other potential work as the future dollars.

The cons in this business are:

- This business highly depends on the seasons. It is a seasonal business unless you have some other things to offer. In the mid-October, when it is winter, the customers go in the hibernation mood as there is nothing much to clean the lawns. In that case, you can offer other services like cleaning the snow to prevent your business come to a standstill.

- To start your business, you will need to fix an amount depending on the type of lawn care business you want to go for. Remember this; you will definitely need equipment and a transportation system to move this equipment from one place to another. For this, you need to be prepared with a fixed amount.

- This business is highly a competitive business. You will find loads of numbers of lawn care business available if you open your phonebook. So, setting up your business among these competitive fields will be a tough one. You may think of cutting some prices from some certain services. Think about the area first before setting up your business. Talk to the existing lawn care companies and try to know about their experiences of working in that area.
- One risk that comes with this type of business is that you can expect to be accused by your customers of breaking lots of things outdoors. Some will insist that you must be the responsible party as you were the last person working in their yard. Ensure the terms of service are clear and leave no room for ambiguities where you might be held liable for thongs you are not responsible for.

- Customers asking or seeking special favors from you outside the signed contract. Some will request that you cut down that small tree branch hanging over the lawn while others will want you to carry away some waste material in your dump van as you leave. In themselves, these little favors are pretty harmless not a big deal really, but they generally slow you down.

When you weigh both the pros and the cons, you will easily find out some basic strong points to ponder on before starting your own lawn care business. You can easily reason your decision on starting the lawn care business of your own. Among all these pros and cons, it is safe to say that if you can work on the cons, you can easily start your own lawn care business with a blast. You can make it a successful and profitable business. Sketch an outline, note down all the necessary steps that you have to consider before starting your business, know everything about the area where you are going to start your business and try to omit all the negative aspects from the list with positivity. In this way, you will be able to set up your own lawn care business in no time.

Now that we have covered what you need to understand in terms of the pros and cons of starting a lawn business, let's turn our attention to other equally important aspects of a lawn care business.

Chapter 1-How to Start Lawn Care Business

If you are thinking about starting a lawn care business then you will require a list of things. These things include basic lawn equipment, physical fitness and advanced knowledge and skills of lawn caring techniques.

Your Goals and Mission Statement
The first step in terms of initiating your new business is identifying exactly what you are aiming to accomplish. Why exactly are you starting your lawn maintenance business? Are you planning to work full-time or part-time? Do you want to manage a team and how big are you planning to grow? Are you well-prepared when it comes to managing the different aspects of the business – sales, marketing, legal, taxes, invoicing? What sets you apart from the local competition? How well-thought-out are your monetary goals for the 1st year? Where do you want to be 5 years down the lane?

Forethought is required for running a lawn care business requires. In the beginning research, the ongoing rates for lawn care to determine whether offering similar rates while still making a profit is possible in your area. It is a smart move to mow lawns in neighborhoods on the same day as scheduled appointments. It's smart to plan to. Writing a solid business plan that includes the reason and type of your business are mandatory to manage the business aspects.

As you define your business goals, start considering creating your own internal mission statement. This assists in clearly defining who you are and clarifying the motivation behind your new lawn management business. It helps to define the purpose to your business. While this step might appear like time wasting and perhaps too corporate-sounding, remember that each time, as you make an important decision, you always can look up your business mission statement and ask yourself whether you are still living up to it. And of course, similar to a Constitution, you can always modify your mission statement as it is a living document.

Select Your Target Market
Goals and mission statement helps in identifying your target market. It is basically the people you are planning to target with your marketing attempts. It can be defined as how the ideal client should look like. For instance, are you mainly targeting your neighborhood or do you want to undertake corporate office clients? Do you intend to open a chain of businesses doing lawn maintenance throughout the district or county? What exact niche do you want to fill?

Generally, marketers choose to develop a buyer persona. It provides an informal snap of the looks of your ideal buyer in one or two short paragraphs. However, developing a buyer persona help create targeted and efficient marketing campaigns.

Determine Your Services
Basically, you need to assess your skills before you start offering your services. It is because you have to be aware of

both your capabilities and disabilities. You have to make sure that you are providing only the services you are capable of offering. It is not a good idea to offer a service you know you lack the equipment or experience necessary for performing it. Otherwise, you will most likely to be sued for accidentally damaging the property of a client. However, the great thing about lawn care business is that you can always build upon a list of services you can provide. With time you can always expand your services as you add up more funding and equipment as well as skills.

Flourish Your Skills
It does not hurt to learn a few kinds of stuff about lawn care services. Basically, anyone can cut grass with a lawn mower. But as you want to charge a professional charge for your lawn care services, you have to prove your capabilities are higher than the neighborhood boy trying to add to his allowance. Even in some cases, you have to do better than the homeowners can do the job themselves. Work on and build up your skills on trimming, mowing, and also edging. This should include handling to cut grass on steep hills and patterned mowing. It will be beneficiary to take a lawn care class if you want to get serious about your business. You can choose any classes at your local community college or just ask around at different greenhouses for tips. However, adding up general plant care on your development list can come in handy. You never know when clients might request info about tending to their plants.

There could be different types of grasses. It depends on various issues as discussed above. If the lawn is going to be used for any type of sporting event then coarse grass should be targeted. On the other hand, fine grasses are the best for any kind of decoration like homecoming party or even wedding. Who likes a wedding ceremony without a lawn anyway? It should be noted that grasses may vary from location to location and you simply cannot do forcefully here. It doesn't matter what type of grass you are looking for, it has to be well-suited with the soil condition and the climate. You don't have to become a soil specialist in this sense, but a little common sense should do the job for you. You can also consider taking some advice from any expert lawn owner. It won't cost you anything. Some people even discover new breeds of grass in the lawn. This task is kind of tricky, but it is up to you whether you want to spend some extra leisure time in thinking about growing it or not. In addition, you can also try changing the colour of the grass of your lawn. A green lawn is the most beautiful, true, but some people opt for changing the colour of the lawn grass by adding some orchids or wildflowers. However, if you are actually liking this idea, you need to make sure you plant those herbs/flowers in a secure passage as you do not want to destroy those while having a morning or evening walk.

Getting Equipment on a Budget
After deciding on developed goals, target market and a mission statement, you need to start buying the equipment you need for running your business. It depends on your goals and the kinds of services you want to provide. Target

equipment is able to get things done faster and professionally with minimal. You can consider making use of the equipment you already have in your house. Shopping around for some used quality equipment can be supplemented by this. Generally, many known people have expensive lawn care equipment lying around without being used. You can offer to use their equipment in the exchange with mowing their lawns or some other work for free on their property.

The best advice to choose the equipment is to network with your peers and dealers. Leverage the Internet to research about the best equipment. Consider the type of included warranty in the equipment and the customer service provided by the dealer. Or you could simply take one step further. You could look for clients that are able to provide your business with equipment in return for a decent discount on their lawns. It will save you the trouble of transporting equipment between clients.

Target lawn equipment capable of assisting to get work done faster (means more jobs done), requires little/minimal maintenance (less time, money lost and fewer replacements) and most importantly, capable of getting the work professionally done (quality service). Carefully consider the total cost of equipment ownership against the initial price. Remember that simply because a lawn mower comes at a cheaper price when purchased outright doesn't necessarily mean it's your best solution. Nonetheless, a regular lawn mower might suffice at starting off as you might have a limited budget.

So how does one go about choosing lawn equipment? Besides networking with your business peers and dealers, leverage on the immense power accorded by the Internet. This will give you a true a feel of the type and quality of equipment you need to achieve your goals. It is also important to think about the type of warranty/guarantee that comes as part of the equipment purchase agreement, the reputation of the dealer and quality of customer service. Don't forget to inquire about the availability of replacement parts.

But once you have managed to establish your business then you will have to consider investing in grade equipment. It will let you and your staffs perform with higher quality work. You might also need other lawn care supplies like weed trimmer, a fertilizer with grass seed.

Transportation Costs
Transportation is one of the major costs involved with the lawn mowing business and the high costs of running a vehicle. It is easier to walk between jobs but not with so much heavy equipment involved. In that case, you have to work in a very small area. Until you can afford a vehicle you can make residents in your and nearby streets offer to mow their lawns at an acceptable price. That way all your jobs will be close together enough for you to get around on foot.

Guidance Information
Make a very good use of the Internet for getting the lawn business startup information. You can get all the info that you

need for free. Look into useful websites that offer a directory of free business resources. Or a better idea is to try and find a mentor in the lawn care organizations. If you have the desire to succeed then you might get an offer for free guidance.

Advertising on a Budget
Basically, no one will come to you for maintaining their lawn if no one is aware of your services. So, if you want to get started in the mowing business then you need to look into the free available advertising methods as you are on a budget. You can create your own ads and take them out. Or you could just pass them out in your neighborhood. Look into having a good use of community notice boards. Sometimes small investments such as car and window decals can help you getting potential clients. If you think it is too expensive then consider a recorded radio ad and playing it at local radio station. It can help your business to boost traffic. Maybe you can walk around your target area and let residents know about your business.

Nowadays you can always make a good use of the Internet. Generate leads from prospects by using different websites in your area. The websites should allow you for a free advertise. You can also email about your lawn care service to everyone in your contact list. If you act like a professional business and budget some money on basic advertising ways, help build brand awareness. Perform giveaways like calendars or stationaries etc. and they will also ensure a positive first impression.

Success is all about undertaking the right type of research, then identifying and employing the right tools in marketing, as well as suitable systems and strategies that help in making beneficial client connections without wreaking havoc on your budget. You need have to have the right service, be there when most suitable and with the right business offer.

Other Startup Disbursals
For some of the startup expenses for your lawn business, you can delay. But waiting too long could end up with unnecessary risks. It is better to establish a legal business structure soon enough to avoid getting into problems. Probable risks include not getting licensed if it is a requirement and not having proper insurance. When you will start earning enough it is important that you start saving money. You can use your saving as reinvestment into the business. By starting out on a budget you will not be able to create a professional looking appearance at start off so you need to invest in marketing and branding for your business.

There are numerous ways to start a lawn mowing service on a budget. Once you get some experience in your business, build up a reputation with the clients. Also, make some savings so you can slowly finance yourself into a more professional appearance.

Licensing Your Business
Permits, tax registrations, and licenses are the important part of starting a business. You need to make sure the starting of

your business is on the right track. As these requirements vary, it is better to ask the local tax revenue office, county clerk, and state department for the types of licenses you are going to need.

For starting a corporation filing paper works are the significant part of the limited liability company. But if you are a sole proprietor of lawn care business, then the kind of form you need filing is a "Doing Business As" paper through the office of county clerk. You can create a business name in this position. You should definitely purchase liability insurance with the help of a lawyer so in the case of an accident you can protect your business. However, policies always vary depending on the provider but you should seriously strongly consider a small business insurance policy.

Evaluate to Learn and Grow
In order to improve your business, you should concentrate on determining how your business is performing as well. It is recommended that you invest in field service software. This software can assist you in managing your client and their information, schedule jobs easily, and automate your billing from the collected data of the fieldwork. Your motive is to get all the helps you can to save your time and get more work done.

Build a Trusted Team
At some point of either initially or as your business grows you need to start building up a team. The team will help you run

your business whether a part-time office worker or a full-time field technician. Finding the right kind of team members can have enormous effect or consequences. Make sure you are appointing someone reliable enough because you might want to avoid getting sued for financial aspects like not paying taxes. It will be very harmful to your business and your reputation.

Knowledge about Climate and Plants

You do not necessarily have to be a climatologist to maintain lawns rather professionally. But it will definitely help you keep lawns first-rated if you choose to have ideas about the seasonal climate conditions of your target area. During the changing of seasons different kinds of grass respond differently. As a result, different techniques are required to keep them healthy year-long. So if you can read up to the knowledge then you will manage healthier and greener lawns. On the plus side, you will have repeated customers in huge numbers.

Winter Plans

Business for lawn care companies in most parts of the country declines during the winter months. But if you plan to offer a snow removal service as well, you will be on the plus side. But in case if you choose not to offer a snow removal service, you can always take off. It depends on how much financially prepared you are. If you are secured enough until spring, you are free to take off.

Staying Updated is the Key
Lawn care business is not rocket science. But as long as there is technological and scientific advancement, any kind of business faces on-going advancement. Likewise, the lawn care industry is also growing with time and developing. Newer kinds of technology and techniques are being developed all the time, research on fertilizer and soil is being advanced. Meanwhile, you might want to continue offering unique and more than average services. So, all you need to do is to stay updated on the industry. You can subscribe to lawn care magazines to stay educated and updated. Since you are acknowledged as a lawn care professional, your clients are most likely expect you to keep their lawns not just cut short but looking fantastic and unique. Advancing with some basic gardening knowledge will do the trick. It will enable you to fix common lawn problems. Whether it is discolored grass or something complex as bare spots, you will know what to do.

Financial Necessities
Another important step is to set up a banking account, business in type. That is because you want to keep your personal and professional finances separate. Also, there are fair chances that it might enable you with little extra money to start your own lawn business. You might take a small business loan or a credit card into consideration if you need to purchase a new lawn mower. The important part is to plan for the times of year mowing lawns is not possible. That is because, in most areas, lawn care is a seasonal business. Snow

shoveling services can help you in the winter season if cold is not a big deal for you. Or you can choose to set a yearly plan for your clients. They can pay in smaller payments for year round.

Chapter 2- How to Get Clients

The lawn care business generally offers a huge load of diversity. Mainly the diversity is in customer types and also in customer services. For this reason choosing to specialize in all the business aspects can help you. But do not forget the customers that are not properly served in your area while you are at it.

Target Client

The actual lawn care you do as the owner of a lawn care service is the single most important component of the standard business day. But there are numerous other details to attend to keep your business smoothly running while paving the path for additional business afterward. Finding clients takes up strategies in all kinds of businesses. Most lawn care businesses fail because of undervaluing their services or chasing the wrong clients. All your strategies should include bringing in more profitable customers. Not only bringing in new clients but also increasing profits from ones you have already served.

Both kinds of clients accordingly should help your business grow. It is a service that someone always needs regardless of the economic conditions you are in. To build your business with referrals from satisfied clients your line of work is to convince those who need it that they need it from your business.

Define Your Business for Clients

You need to identify your business before you can identify your target client. You can start from identifying your top most productive services. Most business owners have an identity crisis while doing all things they are asked to do because they just need the business running.

So when a customer asks a question that starts with can you do, most new landscapers will reply positively without being aware if they have the specialty. But agreeing to a job you have no experience with ends up in training on the job. As a result, the job takes more than estimated time. It ends in unhappy client and spoils your business brand and reputation. If you do not know how to do the job, your customer will know. That is because it will not appear like you know what you are doing. You will only lose a repeat client having a high chance of being a possible referral. So you will have to look at a better way.

When you are starting off with less than a 20" mower and a rake, it is obvious that you will not be specializing in mowing golf courses. So plan to sit down to plan ahead and make a list of top most profitable services.

Look at square footage and think what you do really well with the equipment. Then consider resources that you currently have like suppliers of plants, sprinklers, and trimming. Calculate whether your estimates are accurate and if the jobs profitable and below your capabilities.

Enduring the Storm
You will have the days when the sun is shining brightly but still, you cannot mow or prune. When grasses are wet there is not much you can do really. You can catch up on paperwork, check emails and read over equipment pamphlets. Basically, that is the reason why many lawn service providers choose to work five working days. You can follow their footsteps and save your weekends just in case. You never know when on your work plans the weather wreaks havoc. You can work longer hours alternatively on a regular working day to catch up.

Nevertheless, you can take advantage of another weather phenomenon. Snow plowing can work as a sideline to add to your lawn business. It can prove to be a very lucrative mainstay for that matter. However, a snow removal service does not cost much to launch. You will need to have only a snow blade and you are good to go. You can keep it for your mower or truck and as well as some extra advertising attempts. The best part is that the service offer will provide a regular income stream even during the winter.

Advertise to Attract Clients
People technically buy benefits and not services. It is common for you to have this overwhelming desire to tell the client all about your business company. But actually what the main concern of the customer is, if you can fix the problem they have for their affordable price. Every one of your advertising should deal with solving problems of the clients. But it should not have the purpose of bragging about you. Your ads should induce a client to help in that effort. It should have the power

that customer will pick up the phone and call you. You can use limited time offers classes for providing information or just a simple discount as a weapon to attract more clients.

You need to know how many contacts it will take for you to make a sale so if you do not challenge yourself you will never know.

Working Smarter Not Harder
You can improve once you have identified the most profitable services and the clients that should benefit from them. Using traditional advertising should cost less and produce more qualified clients if you advertise to a specific target market. Once you have ensured a number of clients then you will have an opportunity. It will let you upsell additional services and products. And they will raise the average sale besides building a cushion in your while improving your ultimate outcome. From every contact, as you learn from will let you move the average closing ratio to eight to 10 clients.

Although many operators of lawn management services opt to confine their activities to the summer and spring seasons taking a break in winter, you can turn yours into a year-round service by offering other miscellaneous services such as snow removal and raking leaves. Ensure that your special services get prominent mention on your website and all promotional materials. It's also a prudent business idea good idea to mail your existing clients reminding them that you are only a simple phone call away.

Time Management

As the proprietor and manager of a lawn management service, probably the most single important aspect of your routine business day will be the actual lawn work and care you do. But you will, in addition, be required to give your attention to a variety of other details that contribute to keeping your business operating smoothly and paving the way for more business in the days ahead. Wasting time to manage non-valid customers when you can concentrate on qualified customers can be a foolish move. Concentrating on your target clients will accomplish more jobs in the same amount of time. Define yourself in your business and define your customer. Creating a contacting process to sell benefits is the expression of working smartly but not harder.

A bigger chunk of your valuable time will be taken up by general office administration. This includes routine tasks such as returning customer phone calls/visits, handling the business finances (accounts payable/receivable), instructing your employees, work rescheduling due to weather changes and getting the invoices out. Getting timely payments should be quite straightforward and should ideally not take too much time. Tension can easily build if your customers are not responding in a timely manner to invoices due to personal issues and this could easily damage business relationships.

One way of avoiding client personal problems sneaking into your business is to have them submit a verified credit card number, even when they normally pay by check. Try and entice your clients to enroll in some automated, electronic, flat monthly rate billing program. This eliminates paper-based invoices or having to wait for paper checks to be prepared and dispatched to your office. Even when they fail to send the check on the agreed date, they will automatically be charged through their credit cards.

The most part of your time might be just spent on the phone, to begin with. There are a number of jobs to handle over the phone. They include scheduling jobs, talking to salespeople and marketing. You need to remember to stay organized as it is the essential part. You can choose to do this with either software or notebooks. If you have access to laptop or tablet computers then it is better to do this electronically. You can divide your categories as per the types of your clients with related proximity and logistics. You will be able to see your expenses and income accordingly. You can also plan your service ideas and social networking channels. Recording details are very important in a business. As you are starting out fresh, you will only have a few clients. But if you build up the habit from the beginning, it will pay off later. You will find this habit is hugely helping you put your facts straight and useful at the times of your need.

There is one more advantage of keeping good records. The good reason why you should always map out the details lies into providing service to all customers located in the same area roughly. The records of the types and sizes of the jobs and their locations will let you group a number of mowing jobs. You will be able to keep from wasting your valuable time without crisscrossing your target area. A monthly planner should suffice. The popular software Microsoft Office has a useful monthly calendar template included with Word. So, if you prefer to keep your appointments electronically then you can use that. Or simply there are available apps from Google that synchronize with all your electronic devices to keep electronic calendars. That way you can keep records on your phone and save them as events with notifications.

Marketing

To some degree, all marketing methods work but to rely on just a single one can greatly harm what you get back on your investment in marketing. Every impression you get counts as it contributes to building awareness and in generating faster leads. That's why I advise that you to embrace several marketing strategies for your lawn business. The trick lies in identifying what strategy works best for your business, and developing a suitable mix. Sure, there could be something to learn and pick from your competitors but try and be unique.

Today, you need to be aware that consumers are greatly overwhelmed by the amount of communication being received daily. To stand out, you must be unique. Don't just copy your rivals or what someone else is doing for that will simply make you one of them. The flipside is that when you are just like your competition, price will tend to become the game changer. Bear in mind for you to succeed it will have to be the outcome of many factors, simply not due to advertising. Many of the success factors only get complimented by your efforts at marketing and adverting.

It is the belief of some professionals is that the time you spend building up the base of clients in the first couple of years should be equivalent to that of actual lawn care. It will let you grow the option to be selective about the types of clients you need. So, marketing and advertising need your attention. Spend quality time on these two important aspects every once in a while. What you need to know about advertising is that you need to plan ahead for later services. That is the advertising for summer services should be taken out in the spring. It is the start of the regular mowing season so you need to plant the seed of your business at that period. Similarly, winter services such as snow removal should be taken out in late fall. Do not miss out on your magnetic business card. That way whenever the snow will come down, you can be on your feet. Occasionally as a surprise, you might hear about great advertising opportunities. You should not be too naïve to miss the opportunity. But you will need to have to spend a bit more of your time producing a new ad.

Take Initiatives In Favor Of the Customers
General office administration works tend to take up a lot of your valuable time. But the general motto of your business should be getting paid for your services without any complexity and wasting time. If customers fail to respond to invoices timely then it can build tension. It can also harm your relationship with your clients. That is because sending second or third notices are responsible for creating unnecessary friction. However, life can be complex and your clients might be caught up in difficult situations like tough financial times or simply just too busy. Whichever it is but none of those should become your problem. And you have to make sure that they do not.

The idea is to enroll your clients in an electronic automatic billing. The monthly rate program will let you skip invoices or waiting for checks. You can also have it very genuine if you want to apply hard copies to bear an actual paper invoice. When you just have a handful of clients, in the beginning, using a preprinted invoice from your local office supply store should suffice. Leave them inside the screen door or rubber band it to the knob. The simplest idea is to keep the invoice forms in your vehicle and handwrite the bill at every client's door. It is not mandatory to speak to your clients during passing your bills. The customers, in fact, will probably appreciate that you skipped interrupting for handing over just a bill. But remember not to leave your bill in the mailbox as it is considered private property. Only USPS carrier can use it for delivering mail other than that any other use of it is illegal.

Leverage Your Customers
To start marketing efforts the most cost-effective way to the best customers to grow a new business is through words. Do not have a second thought to ask customers to write a testimonial. But as today's days are the days of social media. So make a good use of social media as well. Use Facebook, Twitter, and social media to tell your friends about your business. If your clients are happy with your work then most of them will take the time to recommend you.

However, to generate referrals you can take it a step further. You may hold a contest to find out who can generate the most referrals and plan a gift to motivate them. You can create a small field team to send gift packages. Make sure they contain your business cards and posters. Always pack some extra stickers and such so your clients can give to their friends and family. Also when you are advertising on social media and websites, generate a new business technique. Offer a discount to customers who agree to give you a work review. Never forget to track your activities as it will let you know which clients are the most profitable ones. Making sure of them will enable you to improve your future marketing efforts.

Another useful business technique is the "Adopt Loss Leader" approach. What does the loss leader approach entail? Essentially, it means giving away something in the hope that you can snag a client for life. Examples of 'leading with loss' include offering a promotion whereby you can even give lawn treatment at a rate that is heavily subsidized or give for free the first month of lawn mowing. Though your revenues are likely to be low initially, your goal should be focused on long-term accounts and perpetual income.

Chapter 3- Earn Money in Off Season Lawn Business

Though it has been stated earlier that the lawn business is a seasonal business that necessarily doesn't mean you stop the business in the off-season. There are ways to maintain your lawn care business during the off-season too. You have to look for the other demands of your customers during this off season period. You have to generate work by satisfying the customers' all the other needs during the cold months. For doing these, extra equipment is needed but the revenue will cover the cost of the extra equipment. Make an outlet by listing all the extra service that your company will be providing for the colder season and try to notify all your customers about it by sending it to them. You can even increase your customer base by providing them a discount on some certain services.

You can expand your business by covering some extra works in the landscape field according to your customers' needs. In the winter, when there is snow everywhere you can think of removing snow as a part of your off-season lawn business. Streets are cleared by city office from the snow, but the sidewalks and driveways are the responsibility of the homeowners. Because of the snow, it is really difficult to take proper care of their lawns too. In this case, your business can save their day by being the rescuer of this snowy situation. Make your customer aware of your snow-clearing service by sending them emails or any outlets.

Lawns need to be taken care of in the spring season when it is the eve of the new arrival amongst the nature. For the upcoming growing season, lawns have to be prepared to welcome the new growths. Lawn care business can offer their services to remove all the extra unwanted straws from the soil that can harm the plants. You can also apply pre-emergency weed killer. You can also offer your customer of cleaning containers and pots. You can start refilling all the pots with soils and start replanting. You can even expand your lawn business by offering services for their indoor plants too. Among other services, you can also think of some offers to give to your customers, like- digging and planning new borders, removal of trees or bushes, clearing all the dead leaves of the winter, fertilizing the plants etc.

The lawn care business can even offer its customers a fall cleaning service, where during the fall, you can satisfy your customers by cleaning the laws from weeds and dry leaves, cleaning the gutters, cleaning the exterior furniture from dust and moving them into an inside place.

During the holidays, houses and roads are dolled up with colorful lights to enjoy the festive mood altogether. However, it is really not an easy job to remove the lights out from its places. It is definitely a tough job. You can offer a helping hand here to make the job easy for your customers. Lawn care business can expand its service section by offering a helping hand to fix out these lights after the holidays are over, especially after Christmas holidays.

There are several ways of forging a profitable business in either commercial or residential lawn maintenance by adding different value-adding services to your core lawn management. Some of these fields may demand more than a mere love of simple gardening if you are to succeed as they may also require some formal education and experience.

The major paths for a career in lawn maintenance and landscaping include:

Gardener/Groundskeeper: This may entail keeping up lawn or garden appearances. You may be called to care of plants as well as other greenery in the yard. Occasionally, you may perform some work in a flower garden, or even n a greenhouse. Here the core task is tending existing yards or landscapes, although it may also require applying herbicides and pesticides, undertaking fall and spring cleanups. Such services may demand you get some good working knowledge of different aspects of horticulture and plants.

Interior landscaper: You can create a profitable channel by caring for plants in shopping malls, office buildings, and other public places. These would be like trimming plants, general care, and maintenance. Often an interior landscaper gives advice on selecting plants and other services loosely related to plant life. Here it helps to have a sharp eye for plant shape, color, texture, and form.

Lawn Spraying: Lawns are exposed constantly to the elements – wind, sunshine, rain, and others such as weeds, insects, and diseases. They are in constantly in decline. To halt the decline, they need protection from such external factors and a regular shot of fertilizer every now and then. Somebody has got to do that and that offers your lawn management business an additional revenue stream. Ensure that you have acquired the best and latest when it comes to spraying equipment and that you are well-versed with local environmental issues and safety concerns. Let your regular customers know you also offer such additional and unique services. Make sure your marketing pieces also contain and highlight the details of your services that are not generally provided by other businesses.

Of course, to your lawn management business, you can add lots of other value-adding services. The options are endless and all it demands is some innovation and enterprise, and you could find yourself into something quite big, especially during the low-season. The key lies in identifying what is needed by customers and stepping in to fill that gap.

Conclusion

To start up and run a successful lawn management business is not nuclear science. Of course, you need to be well-prepared and there are several things that you must know. The good news, however, is that with my comprehensive tips, guides and in-depth analysis of what you need to know and do, this kind of business venture becomes a walk in the park. If you want evidence of how lucrative the business can be, just check around and see the number of upcoming young business executives who are already thriving in this growing industry, once regarded as the preserve of retired and older people. It doesn't require excess funds, but as you start, you could really do with my above analysis if you want to run a successful lawn management company.

Earning money is easy, but with the lawn business, some of you might find it very challenging. A tiny, little careless step may put you in extreme trouble both mentally and financially. However, if you know how to crack the 'lawn business' code, you will be much benefitted. Most importantly, starting the business won't cost you a fortune, but will certainly create a fortune if you are brave enough. All of us know that fortune always favors the brave. So what are you waiting for?

Thank You for Choosing this book! If you need to know how to take care of your lawn, please check out my book Lawn Care (John Baker) on Amazon.com! Thanks!

www.ingramcontent.com/pod-product-compliance
Lightning Source LLC
Chambersburg PA
CBHW061451180526
45170CB00004B/1662